Predators

AFRICAN WILD DOGS

BY MEGAN GENDELL

WWW.APEXEDITIONS.COM

Copyright © 2024 by Apex Editions, Mendota Heights, MN 55120. All rights reserved. No part of this book may be reproduced or utilized in any form or by any means without written permission from the publisher.

Apex is distributed by North Star Editions:
sales@northstareditions.com | 888-417-0195

Produced for Apex by Red Line Editorial.

Photographs ©: Shutterstock Images, cover, 13, 16–17, 20, 22–23, 24, 25, 26–27; iStockphoto, 1, 4–5, 6–7, 8–9, 10–11, 12, 14–15, 18–19, 29

Library of Congress Control Number: 2023909751

ISBN
978-1-63738-770-2 (hardcover)
978-1-63738-813-6 (paperback)
978-1-63738-894-5 (ebook pdf)
978-1-63738-856-3 (hosted ebook)

Printed in the United States of America
Mankato, MN
012024

NOTE TO PARENTS AND EDUCATORS

Apex books are designed to build literacy skills in striving readers. Exciting, high-interest content attracts and holds readers' attention. The text is carefully leveled to allow students to achieve success quickly. Additional features, such as bolded glossary words for difficult terms, help build comprehension.

TABLE OF CONTENTS

CHAPTER 1
WILD DOGS ATTACK 4

CHAPTER 2
FAST AND FURRY 10

CHAPTER 3
TEAM HUNTING 16

CHAPTER 4
PACK LIFE 22

COMPREHENSION QUESTIONS • 28
GLOSSARY • 30
TO LEARN MORE • 31
ABOUT THE AUTHOR • 31
INDEX • 32

CHAPTER 1

WILD DOGS ATTACK

A group of African wild dogs roam the **savanna**. They spot a **herd** of antelopes. The dogs run toward the herd.

African wild dogs sometimes sneak up on other animals. They start to run when they get close.

One antelope is weak. It cannot keep up with the herd. The dogs surround it and attack. Their sharp teeth tear into it.

FAST FACT

When African wild dogs kill an animal, the youngest dogs eat first. The adults wait.

African wild dogs often chase animals that are sick or wounded. Those animals are easier to catch.

The dogs eat quickly and quietly. That way, other animals will not steal their **prey**. Then the dogs move on.

African wild dogs usually hunt at least once a day.

FOOD FOR ALL

Some African wild dogs cannot hunt. They might be too young. Or they might be hurt. To get food, these dogs **whine** and lick the hunters' faces. The hunters throw up the food they ate and share it.

CHAPTER 2

FAST AND FURRY

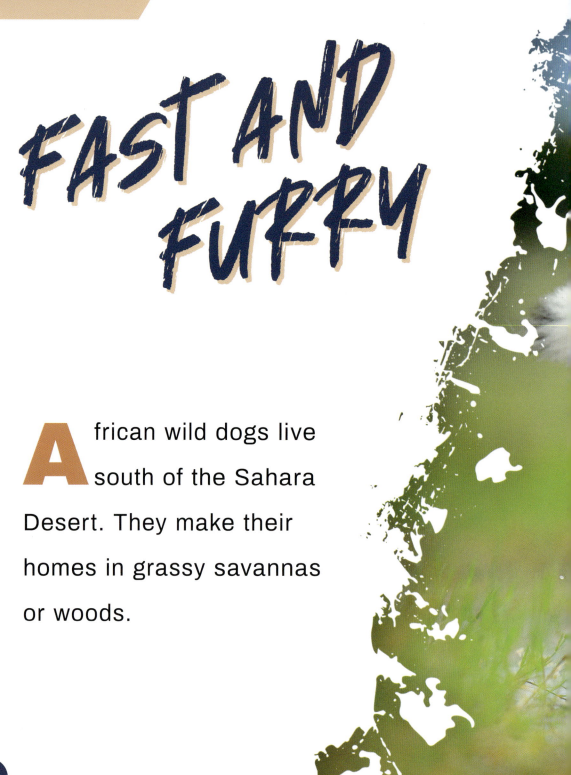

African wild dogs live south of the Sahara Desert. They make their homes in grassy savannas or woods.

10

African wild dogs usually weigh between 40 to 80 pounds (18 to 36 kg). They are about 30 inches (76 cm) tall.

The dogs' fur has patches of different colors. Each dog has a unique fur pattern. No two are the same. The dogs also have large ears. They can hear prey from far away.

The dogs' big ears release heat. That helps them stay cool.

African wild dogs are sometimes called painted dogs. The name comes from the patterns on their fur.

FOLLOW ME

African wild dogs have white tips on their tails. Older dogs raise their tails high in tall grass. Young dogs can easily follow along.

African wild dogs have long and powerful legs. They also have big lungs. As a result, they can chase prey for miles.

African wild dogs are in the same family as wolves, coyotes, and foxes.

FAST FACT

Some African wild dogs can run more than 44 miles per hour (71 km/h).

CHAPTER 3

TEAM HUNTING

African wild dogs are **carnivores**. They often hunt antelopes. They may also eat wildebeests or zebras.

African wild dogs usually catch prey on four out of every five hunts.

African wild dogs can catch animals more than five times their size.

Dogs usually work together to hunt. A few dogs chase the prey up close. When those dogs get tired, new ones take over. They wear out the prey.

FAST FACT

Dogs often bark and sneeze before a hunt. These actions show they're ready to chase prey.

Hunting usually happens around sunrise and sunset. There is enough light to see. But it is dark enough so the dogs blend in with the grass.

FACING DANGER

African wild dogs are **endangered**. Some people turn their **habitats** into farms. Others kill the dogs. They worry the dogs will eat their farm animals.

◀ Many wild dogs live in dry, open areas.

CHAPTER 4

PACK LIFE

African wild dogs live in groups called packs. One male and one female lead each pack. Only these leaders **mate** and have babies.

22

A pack of African wild dogs can have up to 20 members.

A few months after mating, females give birth. Pups stay in the **den**. Then after a few months, the young dogs can go out with the pack.

Females give birth to as many as 20 pups at a time.

Pups learn to hunt by following and watching the pack.

HELPING OUT

After giving birth, mothers are tired. They need time to recover. So, pack members bring food to them. The pack can also help watch over pups.

Pups are fully grown after about one and a half years.

Male dogs usually stay with their pack. But when female dogs are about two years old, they leave. They find groups of males and start new packs.

FAST FACT

African wild dogs usually live for 10 to 12 years in the wild.

COMPREHENSION QUESTIONS

Write your answers on a separate piece of paper.

1. Write a few sentences describing how African wild dogs hunt.

2. If you were an African wild dog, would you want to be a pack leader? Why or why not?

3. How long do pups stay in dens?
   - **A.** just a few days
   - **B.** a few months
   - **C.** about two years

4. How would blending in with grass help African wild dogs hunt?
   - **A.** Their prey would not see them coming.
   - **B.** They could hide from other African wild dogs.
   - **C.** They would not have to chase prey.

5. What does **unique** mean in this book?

*Each dog has a **unique** fur pattern. No two are the same.*

    A. very common
    B. unlike any other
    C. hard to see

6. What does **recover** mean in this book

*After giving birth, mothers are tired. They need time to **recover**.*

    A. run around
    B. rest and get better
    C. hide

Answer key on page 32.

GLOSSARY

carnivores
Animals that eat meat.

den
The home of a wild animal.

endangered
In danger of dying out forever.

habitats
The places where animals normally live.

herd
A large group of animals that live together.

mate
To form a pair and come together to have babies.

prey
An animal that is hunted and eaten by another animal.

savanna
A flat, grassy area with few or no trees.

whine
To make high-pitched sounds.

TO LEARN MORE

BOOKS

Down, Kieran. *Dingo vs. Kangaroo*. Minneapolis: Bellwether Media, 2022.

Humphrey, Natalie. *Jackals in the Wild*. New York: Gareth Stevens Publishing, 2023.

Sommer, Nathan. *Lion vs. Hyena Clan*. Minneapolis: Bellwether Media, 2020.

ONLINE RESOURCES

Visit **www.apexeditions.com** to find links and resources related to this title.

ABOUT THE AUTHOR

Megan Gendell is a writer and editor. She loves learning and writing about wild animals.

INDEX

A
antelopes, 4, 6, 16

C
carnivores, 16

D
den, 24

E
endangered, 21

F
fur, 12

H
habitats, 10, 21
herd, 4, 6
hunting, 4, 6, 9, 16, 18–19, 21

L
legs, 14

M
mating, 22, 24

P
packs, 22, 24–25, 27
prey, 8, 12, 14, 16, 18–19

S
savanna, 4, 10

ANSWER KEY:
1. Answers will vary; 2. Answers will vary; 3. B; 4. A; 5. B; 6. B